D0728960

IT'S NOT WHAT
you look at
THAT MATTERS,
It's WHAT
you see.

- HENRY DAVID THOREAU

WHICH OF MY
photographs
IS MY *favorite*?

THE ONE I'M GOING
TO TAKE *tomorrow.*

— IMOGEN CUNNINGHAM

PHOTOGRAPHY is a WAY
OF FEELING, OF TOUCHING,
of loving. WHAt you
HAVE CAUGHt on film IS
CAPTURED FOREVER ... It
remembers LITTLE
tHINGS, LONG AFTER
you have FORGOtteN
EVERYtHING.

-AARON SISKIND

BE DARING,
be different,
BE IMPRACTICAL,
BE ANYTHING
that will assert
integrity of purpose
AND IMAGINATIVE
VISION
against
the
PLAY-IT-SAFERS, the
creatures of the
COMMONPLACE,
THE SLAVES OF THE
ORDINARY.
—CECIL BEATON

YOU DON'T *TAKE*
A PHOTOGRAPH.
YOU ASK, QUIETLY, to
BORROW It.
— UNKNOWN

STARE.
IT IS THE WAY to
educate
YOUR EYE. AND MORE.
STARE. PRY. listen,
EAVESDROP.
DIE KNOWING
something.
YOU ARE NOT HERE LONG.
-WALKER EVANS

A GOOD PHOTOGRAPHER
MUST LOVE LIFE
MORE THAN HE DOES
PHOTOGRAPHY.
JOEL STRASSER

YOU DON't
MAKE A PHOTOGRAPH
JUST WITH A CAMERA.
YOU BRING TO THE ACT
OF PHOTOGRAPHY ALL THE
PICTURES YOU HAVE SEEN, THE
BOOKS YOU HAVE READ, THE
MUSIC YOU HAVE HEARD,
THE PEOPLE YOU HAVE
LOVED.

- ANSEL ADAMS

TAKING PICTURES
IS *savoring*
life INTENSELY,

every hundredth
OF A SECOND.
- MARK RIBOUD

DESIGNED & ILLUSTRATED BY LISA CONGDON.

What you do makes a difference. Enjoy the world gently.
Printed with soy inks on chlorine-free paper.

COMPENDIUM®
live inspired.

ISBN 978-1935414766